SURVEY OF LAW LIBRARIES: BEST PRACTICES IN DOCKET SEARCHING

ISBN 978-1-57440-583-5

Contents

THE QUESTIONNAIRE

1. Address

   A. Name
   B. Organization
   C. Title
   D. Country
   E. Email Address
   F. Phone Number

2. Type of law of law library

   A. Law Firm
   B. Corporate
   C. University
   D. Courthouse
   E. Other Government
   F. Other

3. Library staff size

4. Personal age of the survey participant

   A. Under 35
   B. 35-44
   C. 45-54
   D. 55-64
   E. 65+

5. Self-assessed level of familiarity with emerging technologies in the legal sector

   A. I am an expert; technology is what I do
   B. I'm pretty well versed but not an expert
   C. I keep up with what I need for my job
   D. It is not really my thing and I find I rely on others for tech evaluations

6. Gender of the survey participant

   A. Male
   B. Female

7. Educational background of the survey participant

   A. I have an MLIS or MLS
   B. I have an MLIS or MLS and a JD Degree
   C. I have a JD, PHD in Law or Bachelor of Law (LL.B) but not an MLIS or MLA
   D. I do not have either an MLIS or MLS or a law degree but have another degree
   E. I do not have a college or graduate school degree

8. How extensive is the use of Pacer by attorneys and others conducting online searches at your organization?

   A. A great deal
   B. A lot
   C. A moderate amount
   D. A little
   E. None at all

9. Does the library offer video tutorials or other training any of the following?

   A. PACER
   B. State Courts
   C. The US Supreme Court

10. Does your organization have paralegals, librarians or attorneys who specialize in searching court dockets for others? If so, who are they? Do they receive any special training?

11. How much did the library spend on PACER fees in the past year, including fees reimbursed by clients?

12. Does your organization use any of the following services for docket searching?

    A. Bloomberg Law Docket Searching
    B. LexisNexis CourtLink
    C. WestLaw Dockets
    D. FastCase and/or Docket Alarm
    E. Other (please specify)

13. What special info literacy and other measures has the library taken to increase the efficiency of docket searching by your library patrons?

PARTICIPANTS LIST

Alameda County Law Library
Balch and Bingham LLP
Barack Ferrazzano and Kirshbaum
Barclay Damon LLP
Boardman and Clark LLP
Brooklyn Law School Library
Canadian Tax Foundation
Champaign County
Chapman and Cutler
Conyers Dill and Pearman
Court of Justice of the European Union
Crowell and Moring LLP
De La Salle University
Dentons Canada LLP
Duke Law
Elgin Law Association
Elon University School of Law
Fairfax Public Law Library
Fasken Martineau DuMoulin LLP
FCHS
Finnegan
Foley Hoag
Fordham Law School
Frost Brown Todd LLC
Gilbert's LLP
Grayson County Law Library
Holland and Knight
Honigman LLP
Jackson Walker LLP

Kathrine R. Everett Law Library
Kegler Brown Hill + Ritter
Kutak Rock LLP
Law Library Association of St. Louis
Law Society of P.E.I. Library

Lawson Lundell LLP
Lehigh County Law Library
Lieff Cabraser
Lincoln Memorial University Law School
Lyon County Law Library
McCaughtry and Associates, Inc.
Mendocino County Law Library
Miller Johnson
Monterey County Law Library
National Judicial Institute
Native American Rights Fund
New York County District Attorney's Office
NYS Office of the Attorney General
Osler, Hoskin and Harcourt LLP
Paul L . Boley Law Library, Lewis and Clark Law School
SBCLL
Sidley Austin LLP
Snell and Wilmer
State Law Library of Montana
State of Oregon Law Library
Stikeman Elliott
Stites and Harbison
Supreme Court of Canada
Supreme Court of KS. Law Library
The Brattle Group

Thormodsgard Law Library University of North Dakota School of Law
Univ. of Idaho College of Law
University of North Carolina
University of Pavia
University of South Carolina School of Law
University of NE College of Law
Vinson and Elkins LLP
Wilson Sonsini Goodrich and Rosati

Characteristics of the Sample

Type of law of law library

	#
Law Firm	30
Corporate/Other Government/Other	14
University	16
Courthouse	12
Total	72

Library staff size

	#
Less than 3	16
3 - 5	21
6 - 10	19
More than 10	16
Total	72

Personal age of the survey participant

	#
Under 45	15
45-54	27
55 and Over	30
Total	72

Self-assessed level of familiarity with emerging technologies in the legal sector

	#
I am an expert, technology is what I do	4
I'm pretty well versed but not an expert	42
I keep up with what I need for my job	23
It is not really my thing and I find I rely on others for tech evaluations	3
Total	72

Gender of the survey participant

	#
Male	24
Female	48
Total	72

Educational background of the survey participant

	#
I have an MLIS or MLS	37
I have an MLIS or MLS and a JD Degree	24
I have a JD, PHD in Law or Bachelor of Law (LL.B) but not an MLIS or MLA	4
I do not have either an MLIS or MLS or a law degree but have another degree	7
Total	72

SUMMARY OF MAIN FINDINGS

Extent of Use of Pacer

We asked: how extensive is the use of PACER by attorneys and others conducting online searches in your organization?

We gave five potential answers to this multiple choice question, which were: A great deal, a lot, A moderate amount, A little, and None at all. Close to 10% did not answer the question and 18.06% did not use PACER at all and 22.22% used it only a little. However, 19.44% used it a great deal and 12.5%, a lot, while 18.06% used it a moderate amount. Law firms were by far the heaviest users; 30% used it a great deal while 23.33% used it a lot while only 3.33% did not use it at all. Also, younger librarians tended to use it more than older ones; for librarians under age 45, a third used it a great deal while this was true of only 10% of those over age 55.

Interestingly, none of those who considered themselves legal technology experts used PACER at all while nearly 43% of those who considered themselves well versed in legal technology used PACER a great deal or a lot. Another interesting demographic fact; almost all PACER use was by women, of whom more than 41% used it a great deal or a lot vs. only 12.5% for men.

Nature of Training on Pacer Offered by the Law Library

We asked: Does the library offer video tutorials or other kinds of training in the use of PACER?

Only 26.4% of the libraries sampled offered video tutorials or other forms of training for PACER. Training was offered by more than 43% of law firms sampled, but only 12.5% of university law libraries and 21/43% of corporate/government law libraries.

19.44% of those sampled offered video tutorials or other forms of training in State Courts docket searching. Courthouses and university libraries were more likely than law firms to offer this kind of training and men were about twice as likely as women to take on this training.

Only 6.94% of those sampled offered video tutorials or other forms of training in searching the US Supreme Court Docket. Only 3.33% of law firms offered this training vs. 12.5% of universities in the sample.

Pervasiveness of Use of Specialized Information Searchers for Docket Searching Tasks

We asked: Does your organization have paralegals, librarians or attorneys who specialize in searching court dockets for others? If so, who are they? Do they receive any special training? Broken out by type of law of law library

A broad range of arrangements exist for docket searching. Most law firms had some form of non-attorneys handling a good portion of the docket searching; mostly they were paralegals and librarians. However, a few had docketing departments and for others, attorneys handled it on their own.

Library Spending on Fees for PACER

We asked: How much did the library spend (in US$) on PACER fees in the past year, including fees reimbursed by clients?

The overall mean was $7,810 but the median was only $725 and the range was 0 to $50,000. Law firms spent by far the most, a mean of $15,293.44 and a median of $6,000.

Use of Specific Commercial Docket Searching Services: Use of Bloomberg Law Docket Searching

We asked: Does your organization use any of the following services for docket searching? First we asked about Bloomberg Law Docket Searching. A third of the libraries sampled used this service; its use was most common among university law libraries – 81.25% used it. It was second most common among law firm libraries – 30% used it. The larger the library staff, the greater the likelihood of use of Bloomberg Law Docket Searching. Only 12.5% of libraries with a staff of fewer than three (FTE) used Bloomberg Law Docket Searching vs. 62.5% of those with a staff of greater than ten, FTE.

Bloomberg Law Docket Searching was particularly likely to be used by librarians who had both an MLS (or MLIS) and a JD degree; indeed, nearly 71% of those in the sample that fit this description used it vs. only 18.92% of those with just an MLS or MLIS.

Use of Specific Commercial Docket Searching Services: Use of CourtLink

36.11% of those sampled used Lexis' CourtLink. 56.14% of law firm libraries used it, as did 50% of university law libraries.

Use of Specific Commercial Docket Searching Services: Use of WestLaw Dockets

44.44% of those sampled used WestLaw Dockets. More than 53% of law firm libraries and nearly 69% of university law libraries used it. Use was strongly related to staff size, and the larger the library staff the greater the likelihood of use. Also use seemed greater by younger than older library staff; more than 53% of those under age 45 used it vs. only 40% of those 55 and older.

Use of Specific Commercial Docket Searching Services: Use of FastCase and/or Docket Alarm

9.72% of respondents used FastCase and/or Docket Alarm. Use was greatest by university law libraries – 25% of those sampled used it – and by courthouse libraries – 16.67% used it. Use was more common among men than women; 16,17% of the former but only 6.25% of the latter in the sample used it.

Use of Other Services for Docket Searching

Other services used were: Courthouse news, Docket Navigator, Les Machina, Domainweb and Courtdrive.

Special Info Literacy Measures Taken by Law Libraries in Docket Searching

We asked: What special info literacy and other measures has the library taken to increase the efficiency of docket searching by your library patrons?

Responses here varied a great deal. Some libraries restricted training to hand outs and intranet self-help pages; others offered one on one training and workshops. Some considered cost and encouraged PACER use and federal court docket searches as an alternative to paid services. Others directed patrons to services that they felt were the easiest to use, often Bloomberg. Many took advantage of new employee open houses and new employee orientation to include docket searching. Most university libraries offered docket searching segments in their advanced legal research courses.

Table 1.1 How extensive is the use of Pacer by attorneys and others conducting online searches at your organization?

	No Answer	A great deal	A lot	A moderate amount	A little	None at all
Entire sample	9.72%	19.44%	12.50%	18.06%	22.22%	18.06%

Table 1.2 How extensive is the use of Pacer by attorneys and others conducting online searches at your organization? Broken out by type of law of law library

Type of law of law library	No Answer	A great deal	A lot	A moderate amount	A little	None at all
Law Firm	6.67%	40.00%	23.33%	13.33%	13.33%	3.33%
Corporate/Other Government/Other	14.29%	7.14%	7.14%	14.29%	28.57%	28.57%
University	6.25%	6.25%	0.00%	31.25%	43.75%	12.50%
Courthouse	16.67%	0.00%	8.33%	16.67%	8.33%	50.00%

Table 1.3 How extensive is the use of Pacer by attorneys and others conducting online searches at your organization? Broken out by library staff size

Library staff size	No Answer	A great deal	A lot	A moderate amount	A little	None at all
Less than 3	12.50%	18.75%	12.50%	18.75%	0.00%	37.50%
3 - 5	9.52%	23.81%	9.52%	23.81%	19.05%	14.29%
6 - 10	10.53%	21.05%	21.05%	15.79%	21.05%	10.53%
More than 10	6.25%	12.50%	6.25%	12.50%	50.00%	12.50%

Table 1.4 How extensive is the use of Pacer by attorneys and others conducting online searches at your organization? Broken out by personal age of the survey participant

Personal age of the survey participant	No Answer	A great deal	A lot	A moderate amount	A little	None at all
Under 45	13.33%	33.33%	13.33%	13.33%	20.00%	6.67%
45-54	14.81%	22.22%	14.81%	22.22%	14.81%	11.11%
55 and Over	3.33%	10.00%	10.00%	16.67%	30.00%	30.00%

Table 1.5 How extensive is the use of Pacer by attorneys and others conducting online searches at your organization? Broken out by self-assessed level of familiarity with emerging technologies in the legal sector

Self-assessed level of familiarity with emerging technologies in the legal sector	No Answer	A great deal	A lot	A moderate amount	A little	None at all
I am an expert, technology is what I do	25.00%	0.00%	0.00%	0.00%	50.00%	25.00%
I'm pretty well versed but not an expert	7.14%	26.19%	16.67%	21.43%	19.05%	9.52%
I keep up with what I need for my job	13.04%	13.04%	8.70%	17.39%	26.09%	21.74%
It is not really my thing and I find I rely on others for tech evaluations	0.00%	0.00%	0.00%	0.00%	0.00%	100.00%

Table 1.6 How extensive is the use of Pacer by attorneys and others conducting online searches at your organization? Broken out by gender of the survey participant

Gender of the survey participant	No Answer	A great deal	A lot	A moderate amount	A little	None at all
Male	8.33%	12.50%	0.00%	20.83%	41.67%	16.67%
Female	10.42%	22.92%	18.75%	16.67%	12.50%	18.75%

Table 1.7 How extensive is the use of Pacer by attorneys and others conducting online searches at your organization? Broken out by educational background of the survey participant

Educational background of the survey participant	No Answer	A great deal	A lot	A moderate amount	A little	None at all
I have an MLIS or MLS	10.81%	27.03%	18.92%	8.11%	18.92%	16.22%
I have an MLIS or MLS and a JD Degree	4.17%	12.50%	8.33%	33.33%	37.50%	4.17%
I have a JD, PHD in Law or Bachelor of Law (LL.B) but not an MLIS or MLA	50.00%	0.00%	0.00%	25.00%	0.00%	25.00%
I do not have either an MLIS or MLS or a law degree but have another degree	0.00%	14.29%	0.00%	14.29%	0.00%	71.43%

Table 2 Does the library offer video tutorials or other training any of the following?

Table 2.1.1 Does the library offer video tutorials or other PACER training?

	Yes	No
Entire sample	26.39%	73.61%

Table 2.1.2 Does the library offer video tutorials or other PACER training? Broken out by type of law of law library

Type of law of law library	Yes	No
Law Firm	43.33%	56.67%
Corporate/Other Government/Other	21.43%	78.57%
University	12.50%	87.50%
Courthouse	8.33%	91.67%

Table 2.1.3 Does the library offer video tutorials or other PACER training? Broken out by library staff size

Library staff size	Yes	No
Less than 3	37.50%	62.50%
3 - 5	28.57%	71.43%
6 - 10	36.84%	63.16%
More than 10	0.00%	100.00%

Table 2.1.4 Does the library offer video tutorials or other PACER trainings Broken out by personal age of the survey participant

Personal age of the survey participant	Yes	No
Under 45	33.33%	66.67%
45-54	33.33%	66.67%
55 and Over	16.67%	83.33%

Table 2.1.5 Does the library offer video tutorials or other PACER training? Broken out by self-assessed level of familiarity with emerging technologies in the legal sector

Self-assessed level of familiarity with emerging technologies in the legal sector	Yes	No
I am an expert, technology is what I do	25.00%	75.00%
I'm pretty well versed but not an expert	30.95%	69.05%
I keep up with what I need for my job	21.74%	78.26%
It is not really my thing and I find I rely on others for tech evaluations	0.00%	100.00%

Table 2.1.6 Does the library offer video tutorials or other PACER training? Broken out by gender of the survey participant

Gender of the survey participant	Yes	No
Male	29.17%	70.83%
Female	25.00%	75.00%

Table 2.1.7 Does the library offer video tutorials or other PACER training? Broken out by educational background of the survey participant

Educational background of the survey participant	Yes	No
I have an MLIS or MLS	37.84%	62.16%
I have an MLIS or MLS and a JD Degree	16.67%	83.33%
I have a JD, PHD in Law or Bachelor of Law (LL.B) but not an MLIS or MLA	0.00%	100.00%
I do not have either an MLIS or MLS or a law degree but have another degree	14.29%	85.71%

Table 2.2.1 Does the library offer video tutorials or any other training in the use of specific state court dockets?

	Yes	No
Entire sample	19.44%	80.56%

Table 2.2.2 Does the library offer video tutorials or any other training in the use of specific state court dockets? Broken out by type of law of law library

Type of law of law library	Yes	No
Law Firm	13.33%	86.67%
Corporate/Other Government/Other	21.43%	78.57%
University	25.00%	75.00%
Courthouse	25.00%	75.00%

Table 2.2.3 Does the library offer video tutorials or any other training in the use of specific state court dockets? Broken out by library staff size

Library staff size	Yes	No
Less than 3	18.75%	81.25%
3 - 5	19.05%	80.95%
6 - 10	31.58%	68.42%
More than 10	6.25%	93.75%

Table 2.2.4 Does the library offer video tutorials or any other training in the use of specific state court dockets? Broken out by personal age of the survey participant

Personal age of the survey participant	Yes	No
Under 45	20.00%	80.00%
45-54	22.22%	77.78%
55 and Over	16.67%	83.33%

Table 2.2.5 Does the library offer video tutorials or any other training in the use of specific state court dockets? Broken out by self-assessed level of familiarity with emerging technologies in the legal sector

Self-assessed level of familiarity with emerging technologies in the legal sector	Yes	No
I am an expert, technology is what I do	0.00%	100.00%
I'm pretty well versed but not an expert	23.81%	76.19%
I keep up with what I need for my job	17.39%	82.61%
It is not really my thing and I find I rely on others for tech evaluations	0.00%	100.00%

Table 2.2.6 Does the library offer video tutorials or any other training in the use of specific state court dockets? Broken out by gender of the survey participant

Gender of the survey participant	Yes	No
Male	29.17%	70.83%
Female	14.58%	85.42%

Table 2.2.7 Does the library offer video tutorials or any other training in the use of specific state court dockets? Broken out by educational background of the survey participant

Educational background of the survey participant	Yes	No
I have an MLIS or MLS	18.92%	81.08%
I have an MLIS or MLS and a JD Degree	20.83%	79.17%
I have a JD, PHD in Law or Bachelor of Law (LL.B) but not an MLIS or MLA	25.00%	75.00%
I do not have either an MLIS or MLS or a law degree but have another degree	14.29%	85.71%

Table 2.3.1 Does the library offer video tutorials or other the US Supreme Court trainings

	Yes	No
Entire sample	6.94%	93.06%

Table 2.3.2 Does the library offer video tutorials or any other training in the use of the US Supreme court docket? Broken out by type of law of law library

Type of law of law library	Yes	No
Law Firm	3.33%	96.67%
Corporate/Other Government/Other	7.14%	92.86%
University	12.50%	87.50%
Courthouse	8.33%	91.67%

Table 2.3.3 Does the library offer video tutorials or any other training in the use of the US Supreme court docket? Broken out by library staff size

Library staff size	Yes	No
Less than 3	6.25%	93.75%
3 - 5	0.00%	100.00%
6 - 10	21.05%	78.95%
More than 10	0.00%	100.00%

Table 2.3.4 Does the library offer video tutorials or any other training in the use of the US Supreme court docket? Broken out by personal age of the survey participant

Personal age of the survey participant	Yes	No
Under 45	6.67%	93.33%
45-54	11.11%	88.89%
55 and Over	3.33%	96.67%

Table 2.3.5 Does the library offer video tutorials or any other training in the use of the US Supreme court docket? Broken out by self-assessed level of familiarity with emerging technologies in the legal sector

Self-assessed level of familiarity with emerging technologies in the legal sector	Yes	No
I am an expert, technology is what I do	0.00%	100.00%
I'm pretty well versed but not an expert	9.52%	90.48%
I keep up with what I need for my job	4.35%	95.65%
It is not really my thing and I find I rely on others for tech evaluations	0.00%	100.00%

Table 2.3.6 Does the library offer video tutorials or any other training in the use of the US Supreme court docket? Broken out by gender of the survey participant

Gender of the survey participant	Yes	No
Male	12.50%	87.50%
Female	4.17%	95.83%

Table 2.3.7 Does the library offer video tutorials or any other training in the use of the US Supreme court docket? Broken out by educational background of the survey participant

Educational background of the survey participant	Yes	No
I have an MLIS or MLS	5.41%	94.59%
I have an MLIS or MLS and a JD Degree	12.50%	87.50%
I have a JD, PHD in Law or Bachelor of Law (LL.B) but not an MLIS or MLA	0.00%	100.00%
I do not have either an MLIS or MLS or a law degree but have another degree	0.00%	100.00%

Does your organization have paralegals, librarians or attorneys who specialize in searching court dockets for others? If so, who are they? Do they receive any special training? Broken out by type of law of law library

Law Firm

1) no
2) Each service group has 1 or more paralegals who search court dockets.
3) We offer training one-on-one as well as with vendor representatives/trainers for docket searches. No special training unless requested.
4) Most litigation paralegals, legal secretaries and/or library handle for attorneys - we do not have docketing clerks
5) no
6) research lawyers and reference librarians
7) No
8) Yes, litigation paralegals. Training unknown. Court docket searching in Canada is entirely different than in the U.S.
9) We have one litigation paralegal and the librarians that do this. We have all been doing it long enough that special training has not been involved
10) Yes and yes
11) We have a fairly new Docketing department but I believe that's calendaring. Library Services helps search federal and state court dockets for litigation history as part of due diligence efforts, which is a new service I initiated since starting at the firm 6 years ago.
12) no
13) No, we do not have specialists who do only this task.
14) Yes
15) bith, yes
16) The librarians and paralegals search for court dockets. We do not have a docketing department.
17) librarians and paralegals
18) Several paralegals do extensive docket searching for their assigned attorneys. I do all the other docket research for anyone (attorney, paralegal, secretary) who asks
19) Librarian and paralegals do quite a bit of the docket searching. Several attorneys do their own docket searching. Legal assistants pull dockets for attorneys. Training is very informal - may individuals prefer to do it themselves rather than attend a training session.

20) We all pretty much do our own searching at every level. No training for PACER but we do have Westlaw Dockets included in our trainings.
21) No.
22) Paralegals
23) Yes, webinars and experience
24) Not really - we don't practice US law
25) Paralegals, librarians, secretarys
26) yes. Managing clerk's office and paralegals are trained in PACER and PACER pro

Corporate/Other Government/Other

1) One librarian who has a history with court document retrieval and is very familiar with PACER
2) Yes; Librarians and Analysts; Yes, they receive special training
3) Librarians, admns. No special training
4) n/a
5) no
6) No
7) Again, not an appropriate question for Public Law Libraries.
8) Yes, however, I am not involved in that at this time.
9) We don't specialize in searching court dockets.

University

1) No
2) no
3) Librarians. We train with the representative from the company that provides us electronic dockets (we rarely use PACER itself).
4) no
5) No.
6) Yes and no. We do have one librarian that has access to the state dockets. And two librarians that have regularly given trainings on dockets.
7) All dual degreed librarians search court dockets. We run in house training on Pacer and state dockets.
8) no
9) The law librarian does the searching of court dockets. Training on how to search such was received through informal training (like on the job training) from a renowned academic law library in the country.

Courthouse

1) no
2) no. All staff guides users in these areas.
3) no.
4) Reference librarian. No, but he does have a law degree.

5) The reference librarians are trained a whole month to search any kind of legal information. Research questions vary a lot: jurisprudence, historical questions, legislation or regulation, etc. We also have law clerks who do similar researches. The library trains them. I don't think anyone is "specialized" in court dockets, we are all able to the legal research as a whole.

Table 3.1 How much did the library spend (in US$) on PACER fees in the past year, including fees reimbursed by clients?

	Mean	Median	Minimum	Maximum
Entire sample	7810.01	725.00	0.00	50000.00

Table 3.2 How much did the library spend (in US$) on PACER fees in the past year, including fees reimbursed by clients? Broken out by type of law of law library

Type of law of law library	Mean	Median	Minimum	Maximum
Law Firm	15293.44	6000.00	0.00	50000.00
Corporate/Other Government/Other	2693.75	25.00	0.00	12000.00
University	30.56	0.00	0.00	250.00
Courthouse	0.00	0.00	0.00	0.00

Table 3.3 How much did the library spend (in US$) on PACER fees in the past year, including fees reimbursed by clients? Broken out by library staff size

Library staff size	Mean	Median	Minimum	Maximum
Less than 3	6777.78	2500.00	0.00	20000.00
3 - 5	11735.45	4250.00	0.00	47000.00
6 - 10	8822.73	0.00	0.00	50000.00
More than 10	1690.63	2.50	0.00	12000.00

Table 3.4 How much did the library spend (in US$) on PACER fees in the past year, including fees reimbursed by clients? Broken out by personal age of the survey participant

Personal age of the survey participant	Mean	Median	Minimum	Maximum
Under 45	8430.00	10100.00	0.00	20000.00
45-54	7823.08	4000.00	0.00	30000.00
55 and Over	7661.38	12.50	0.00	50000.00

Table 3.5 How much did the library spend (in US$) on PACER fees in the past year, including fees reimbursed by clients? Broken out by self-assessed level of familiarity with emerging technologies in the legal sector

Self-assessed level of familiarity with emerging technologies in the legal sector	Mean	Median	Minimum	Maximum
I am an expert, technology is what I do	2502.50	2502.50	5.00	5000.00
I'm pretty well versed but not an expert	8579.78	2000.00	0.00	47000.00
I keep up with what I need for my job	8481.33	250.00	0.00	50000.00
It is not really my thing and I find I rely on others for tech evaluations	0.00	0.00	0.00	0.00

Table 3.6 How much did the library spend (in US$) on PACER fees in the past year, including fees reimbursed by clients? Broken out by gender of the survey participant

Gender of the survey participant	Mean	Median	Minimum	Maximum
Male	2033.67	0.00	0.00	25000.00
Female	11275.81	4500.00	0.00	50000.00

Table 3.7 How much did the library spend (in US$) on PACER fees in the past year, including fees reimbursed by clients? Broken out by educational background of the survey participant

Educational background of the survey participant	Mean	Median	Minimum	Maximum
I have an MLIS or MLS	10172.64	5000.00	0.00	47000.00
I have an MLIS or MLS and a JD Degree	6585.00	0.00	0.00	50000.00
I have a JD, PHD in Law or Bachelor of Law (LL.B) but not an MLIS or MLA	0.00	0.00	0.00	0.00
I do not have either an MLIS or MLS or a law degree but have another degree	0.00	0.00	0.00	0.00

Table 4 Does your organization use any of the following services for docket searching?

Table 4.1.1 Does your organization use Bloomberg Law Docket Searching?

	Yes	No
Entire sample	33.33%	66.67%

Table 4.1.2 Does your organization use Bloomberg Law Docket Searching? Broken out by type of law of law library

Type of law of law library	Yes	No
Law Firm	30.00%	70.00%
Corporate/Other Government/Other	14.29%	85.71%
University	81.25%	18.75%
Courthouse	0.00%	100.00%

Table 4.1.3 Does your organization use Bloomberg Law Docket Searching? Broken out by library staff size

Library staff size	Yes	No
Less than 3	12.50%	87.50%
3 - 5	28.57%	71.43%
6 - 10	31.58%	68.42%
More than 10	62.50%	37.50%

Table 4.1.4 Does your organization use Bloomberg Law Docket Searching? Broken out by personal age of the survey participant

Personal age of the survey participant	Yes	No
Under 45	26.67%	73.33%
45-54	29.63%	70.37%
55 and Over	40.00%	60.00%

Table 4.1.5 Does your organization use Bloomberg Law Docket Searching? Broken out by self-assessed level of familiarity with emerging technologies in the legal sector

Self-assessed level of familiarity with emerging technologies in the legal sector	Yes	No
I am an expert, technology is what I do	25.00%	75.00%
I'm pretty well versed but not an expert	33.33%	66.67%
I keep up with what I need for my job	39.13%	60.87%
It is not really my thing and I find I rely on others for tech evaluations	0.00%	100.00%

Table 4.1.6 Does your organization use Bloomberg Law Docket Searching? Broken out by gender of the survey participant

Gender of the survey participant	Yes	No
Male	37.50%	62.50%
Female	31.25%	68.75%

Table 4.1.7 Does your organization use Bloomberg Law Docket Searching? Broken out by educational background of the survey participant

Educational background of the survey participant	Yes	No
I have an MLIS or MLS	18.92%	81.08%
I have an MLIS or MLS and a JD Degree	70.83%	29.17%
I have a JD, PHD in Law or Bachelor of Law (LL.B) but not an MLIS or MLA	0.00%	100.00%
I do not have either an MLIS or MLS or a law degree but have another degree	0.00%	100.00%

Table 4.2.1 Does your organization use LexisNexis CourtLink?

	Yes	No
Entire sample	36.11%	63.89%

Table 4.2.2 Does your organization use LexisNexis CourtLink? Broken out by type of law of law library

Type of law of law library	Yes	No
Law Firm	56.67%	43.33%
Corporate/Other Government/Other	7.14%	92.86%
University	50.00%	50.00%
Courthouse	0.00%	100.00%

Table 4.2.3 Does your organization use LexisNexis CourtLink? Broken out by library staff size

Library staff size	Yes	No
Less than 3	18.75%	81.25%
3 - 5	38.10%	61.90%
6 - 10	42.11%	57.89%
More than 10	43.75%	56.25%

Table 4.2.4 Does your organization use LexisNexis CourtLink? Broken out by personal age of the survey participant

Personal age of the survey participant	Yes	No
Under 45	33.33%	66.67%
45-54	37.04%	62.96%
55 and Over	36.67%	63.33%

Table 4.2.5 Does your organization use LexisNexis CourtLink? Broken out by self-assessed level of familiarity with emerging technologies in the legal sector

Self-assessed level of familiarity with emerging technologies in the legal sector	Yes	No
I am an expert, technology is what I do	25.00%	75.00%
I'm pretty well versed but not an expert	45.24%	54.76%
I keep up with what I need for my job	26.09%	73.91%
It is not really my thing and I find I rely on others for tech evaluations	0.00%	100.00%

Table 4.2.6 Does your organization use LexisNexis CourtLink? Broken out by gender of the survey participant

Gender of the survey participant	Yes	No
Male	41.67%	58.33%
Female	33.33%	66.67%

Table 4.2.7 Does your organization use LexisNexis CourtLink? Broken out by educational background of the survey participant

Educational background of the survey participant	Yes	No
I have an MLIS or MLS	37.84%	62.16%
I have an MLIS or MLS and a JD Degree	41.67%	58.33%
I have a JD, PHD in Law or Bachelor of Law (LL.B) but not an MLIS or MLA	0.00%	100.00%
I do not have either an MLIS or MLS or a law degree but have another degree	28.57%	71.43%

Table 4.3.1 Does your organization use WestLaw Dockets?

	Yes	No
Entire sample	44.44%	55.56%

Table 4.3.2 Does your organization use WestLaw Dockets? Broken out by type of law of law library

Type of law of law library	Yes	No
Law Firm	53.33%	46.67%
Corporate/Other Government/Other	21.43%	78.57%
University	68.75%	31.25%
Courthouse	16.67%	83.33%

Table 4.3.3 Does your organization use WestLaw Dockets? Broken out by library staff size

Library staff size	Yes	No
Less than 3	25.00%	75.00%
3 - 5	38.10%	61.90%
6 - 10	52.63%	47.37%
More than 10	62.50%	37.50%

Table 4.3.4 Does your organization use WestLaw Dockets? Broken out by personal age of the survey participant

Personal age of the survey participant	Yes	No
Under 45	53.33%	46.67%
45-54	44.44%	55.56%
55 and Over	40.00%	60.00%

Table 4.3.5 Does your organization use WestLaw Dockets? Broken out by self-assessed level of familiarity with emerging technologies in the legal sector

Self-assessed level of familiarity with emerging technologies in the legal sector	Yes	No
I am an expert, technology is what I do	25.00%	75.00%
I'm pretty well versed but not an expert	54.76%	45.24%
I keep up with what I need for my job	34.78%	65.22%
It is not really my thing and I find I rely on others for tech evaluations	0.00%	100.00%

Table 4.3.6 Does your organization use WestLaw Dockets? Broken out by gender of the survey participant

Gender of the survey participant	Yes	No
Male	41.67%	58.33%
Female	45.83%	54.17%

Table 4.3.7 Does your organization use WestLaw Dockets? Broken out by educational background of the survey participant

Educational background of the survey participant	Yes	No
I have an MLIS or MLS	32.43%	67.57%
I have an MLIS or MLS and a JD Degree	70.83%	29.17%
I have a JD, PHD in Law or Bachelor of Law (LL.B) but not an MLIS or MLA	25.00%	75.00%
I do not have either an MLIS or MLS or a law degree but have another degree	28.57%	71.43%

Table 4.4.1 Does your organization use FastCase and/or Docket Alarm?

	Yes	No
Entire sample	9.72%	90.28%

Table 4.4.2 Does your organization use FastCase and/or Docket Alarm? Broken out by type of law of law library

Type of law of law library	Yes	No
Law Firm	3.33%	96.67%
Corporate/Other Government/Other	0.00%	100.00%
University	25.00%	75.00%
Courthouse	16.67%	83.33%

Table 4.4.3 Does your organization use FastCase and/or Docket Alarm? Broken out by library staff size

Library staff size	Yes	No
Less than 3	0.00%	100.00%
3 - 5	4.76%	95.24%
6 - 10	10.53%	89.47%
More than 10	25.00%	75.00%

Table 4.4.4 Does your organization use FastCase and/or Docket Alarm? Broken out by personal age of the survey participant

Personal age of the survey participant	Yes	No
Under 45	13.33%	86.67%
45-54	3.70%	96.30%
55 and Over	13.33%	86.67%

Table 4.4.5 Does your organization use FastCase and/or Docket Alarm? Broken out by self-assessed level of familiarity with emerging technologies in the legal sector

Self-assessed level of familiarity with emerging technologies in the legal sector	Yes	No
I am an expert, technology is what I do	25.00%	75.00%
I'm pretty well versed but not an expert	9.52%	90.48%
I keep up with what I need for my job	8.70%	91.30%
It is not really my thing and I find I rely on others for tech evaluations	0.00%	100.00%

Table 4.4.6 Does your organization use FastCase and/or Docket Alarm? Broken out by gender of the survey participant

Gender of the survey participant	Yes	No
Male	16.67%	83.33%
Female	6.25%	93.75%

Table 4.4.7 Does your organization use FastCase and/or Docket Alarm? Broken out by educational background of the survey participant

Educational background of the survey participant	Yes	No
I have an MLIS or MLS	10.81%	89.19%
I have an MLIS or MLS and a JD Degree	12.50%	87.50%
I have a JD, PHD in Law or Bachelor of Law (LL.B) but not an MLIS or MLA	0.00%	100.00%
I do not have either an MLIS or MLS or a law degree but have another degree	0.00%	100.00%

Other:

1. Courthouse News
2. We have looked at all of these but our main focus is not the US. Bloomberg was the best.
3. Docket Navigator, Lex Machina
4. Law360; None for market research purposes.
5. specific courts' websites
6. Courthouse News Service
7. docket navigator
8. Court Services Online (BC government service); Westlaw Litigator
9. Courtdrive and PACER and state specific subscriptions
10. SOQUIJ (Quebec), court websites
11. Domainweb
12. We do not do docket search
13. I am not sure

What special info literacy and other measures has the library taken to increase the efficiency of docket searching by your library patrons? Broken out by type of law library

Law Firm

1) Training on Courtlink for secretaries
2) How state and federal courts are organized via on-board training of new staff
3) Just keep trying to get the word out that we can help with training and efficiency
4) User guides on intranet pages
5) none, the library does the searching
6) Not applicable to a Canadian firm.
7) Encouraging them to contact us if they can't find a docket and use PACER for federal court dockets as a cost-effective strategy rather than using Westlaw/CourtLink.
8) Tax court dockets available in Thomson Reuters Canadian tax resource (Taxnet Pro) mined for regularly reporting to the tax department.
9) Handouts, articles, and open houses
10) Offer training at new hire orientations, occasionally attend paralegal meetings, standing offer for training on any online resources.
11) none
12) We use PacerPro to help prevent paying twice for documents that multiple people access.
13) Training
14) training
15) training on CSO and Litigator
16) e-mails, training video available on firm intranet, personal training sessions, promote CourtLink sessions with dedicated vendor educator
17) I do offer to cover PACER and WL docket searching by many individuals "train" themselves.
18) Offered Westlaw training videos, but mostly just remind people of least expensive resource for their particular needs.
19) None.
20) training and products like pacerpro

Corporate/Other Government/Other

1) Training
2) 1:1 training
3) One on One lessons with patrons who request assistance.

University

1) Training with Bloomberg Law Docket Searching, direct training, support, and docket research for our legal clinics
2) None.
3) provide instruction and training
4) None that I know of.
5) directed patrons to Bloomberg Law because of its ease of use
6) Training for students in Advanced Legal Research, noontime sessions, and upper level classes.
7) Teach docket searching in our Legal Research III class
8) Teach students how to use docket searching in Bloomberg Law.
9) We have a research guide.
10) It is included in our Advanced Legal Research Courses.
11) involvement in Legal Writing and Research, specific class on practice oriented IT, and involvement in faculty research.

Courthouse

1) none
2) no specific program for pro se users
3) none
4) None so far, but that would be interesting to see what we could do about it.
5) Nothing

Made in United States
North Haven, CT
04 November 2026

21727478R00026